"[Alcalá] uses empty spaces, hesitations, and semantic difficulties to address mothers and daughters, herself as mother and herself as daughter, and the messy emotions and miscommunications that move between languages (in her case, English and Spanish), as well as between and within female bodies, in breastfeeding, menstruation, giving birth. Alcalá's short, wry lines, self-interruptions, and open spaces remind us how little precedent there is for honest writing on these topics, compared with the epic traditions of fathers and sons."　　　　　**—Stephanie Burt,** *The New York Times*

"How do we trace shifts of home or syllable, the history of becoming in language? We show what's passed on with the mother-milk, the blood-words, pushed from the body onto the page. That's what these poems do, spilling beautifully, forming in the mouth of the reader. This is the 'ark built to survive': our things built with words circling, mother-to-daughter-to-mother-to-daughter."　　　　　**—Eleni Sikelianos**

"Here are poems that reckon with the histories of family, generations, language, and love: how our tongues are mothered or not, how we are given to and abandoned. Alcalá writes, 'What good is it to erect/ of absence/ a word?' Tough and gorgeous, smart and touching, these poems are offerings that tie, untie, unite, entice."　　　　　**—Hoa Nguyen**

"Rosa Alcalá's new poemario *MyOTHER TONGUE* begins in the archives of what has yet to be written. She writes with precision and dynamism from the borders between death (of a mother) and birth (of a daughter). What a body produces, and what produces a body: labor, trauma, memory, sacrifice, pain, danger, and language formed both on the tongue and in the culture and the spaces between what can be said and what is missing, the linguistic and existential problem of not having the right words. The darknesses in Alcalá's work emerge from what happens when we don't see ourselves in the languages that both form and destroy us as we labor in this 'dream called money.' Alcalá is a {un}documentarian of the highest order, a {un}documentarian of what history and memory try to erase. Her poems are urgent, demanding, and haunting."　　　　　**—Daniel Borzutzky**

Praise for *The Lust of Unsentimental Waters*

"*The Lust of Unsentimental Waters* is a playful and rigorous book that attempts to uncover the evolving and sometimes Oz-like machinations of late capitalism . . . At every juncture, [Alcalá] is wry and brilliant in her attempt to uncover where hierarchies are born."

—Carmen Giménez, Poetry Foundation

"'I want to know how everything changes with the price of admission,' writes Rosa Alcalá in her extraordinary new book. These poems begin at the exact point where 'the fundamental concepts of elementary navigation / become unhinged,' as they invent a new way of talking—developing tenuous and affectionate convergences between desire and fear, love and anger—even sex, money, tradition, and the history of appearances. It's all here. What fascinates Alcalá is precisely what animates her poetry—'the mess of lost power,' compelled at once by contradiction and complicity, yet cleaving with an unsentimental eye and an inspiring wit."

—Joshua Marie Wilkinson

Praise for *Undocumentaries*

"Rosa Alcalá, originally from Paterson, NJ, is a true daughter of W.C. Williams, with a distinct, gutsy, and penetrating identity twining a public poiesis with her own luminous particulars. I know of no one else writing such poems that cut into and reenact the 'plebeian' with such personal force, eloquence, and skill."

—Anne Waldman

"If poetic episodes can act as gauges of social role-playing and role-disruption, what might lie 'outside' the roles 'we' 'inhabit?' What remains undocumented, but hardly silent? What are the sensed and projected traces of 'identity' that are ideologically eviscerated, and minimally verifiable? Rosa Alcalá calls up a most magical theater when exploring these quandaries. The tipping (flash) points she constructs continuously build up toward the (touched, handled, engaged) experiential moment, all the while resisting an object-status art. This is a poetics that's prologue + epilogue to incidence, and never the 'it' itself. Sweet tin on tawny brass, flesh-toned, radio-worthy."

—Rodrigo Toscano

YOU

YOU

ROSA ALCALÁ

COFFEE HOUSE PRESS
Minneapolis
2024

Coffee House Press books are available to the trade through our primary distributor, Consortium Book Sales & Distribution, cbsd.com or (800) 283-3572. For personal orders, catalogs, or other information, write to info@coffeehousepress.org.

Coffee House Press is a nonprofit literary publishing house. Support from private foundations, corporate giving programs, government programs, and generous individuals helps make the publication of our books possible. We gratefully acknowledge their support in detail in the back of this book.

LIBRARY OF CONGRESS CATALOGING-IN-PUBLICATION DATA

Names: Alcalá, Rosa, author.
Title: You / Rosa Alcalá.
Description: Minneapolis : Coffee House Press, 2024.
Identifiers: LCCN 2023039640 (print) | LCCN 2023039641 (ebook) |
    ISBN 9781566897013 (paperback) | ISBN 9781566897020 (e-book)
Subjects: LCGFT: Poetry.
Classification: LCC PS3601.L34256 Y68 2024 (print) | LCC PS3601.L34256
    (ebook) | DDC 811.6—dc23/eng/20230828
LC record available at https://lccn.loc.gov/2023039640
LC ebook record available at https://lccn.loc.gov/2023039641

PRINTED IN THE UNITED STATES OF AMERICA

31 30 29 28 27 26 25 24   1 2 3 4 5 6 7 8

Table of Contents

You started that night in a straightforward way. You began by trying to remember. You tried to "flush her out" by telling a story that would be so painful she would still feel it. If she felt it, then you could consider you had bridged the gap of years.

—DAVID ANTIN TO ELEANOR ANTIN ABOUT HER PERFORMANCE

To unravel a torment you must begin somewhere.

—LOUISE BOURGEOIS, FROM *WHAT IS THE SHAPE OF THIS PROBLEM?*

YOU

How It Started, How It's Going {An Introduction}

I rose from sleep one night, my back a trouble tense, and rode in reverse
from the idiopathic to what I believed were the glories

each scene an indulgence of a body I possessed.

One was carried above other bodies, hovered over them, was weightless.

Another threaded itself, a quarter of two couples, in intricate maneuvers.
Switched dance partners easily.

Or stumbled with a stranger to his place.   I watched over her
waited for the sun to come up

and while I was looking out the window
she left, became older

went to sleep next to her (our) dying mother.

Together we listened to the rattle become more foreign than any accent
until it was pure accent, meaning

inaudible.

It took so little time to get from the walk-up to the hospital.

I was trying to write a book about my mother
and the bodies were trying to get away from her,
seeking pleasure.

With my contested middle-aged body I carried them away from pleasure
to this place,
to map where fear begins
for girls, for women.

What I mean to say is that this book is still about my mother

that in the absence of her I mothered myself all over again with worry,
which is how I mother.

I spoke to myself, the only recourse when you're
invisible.

But then I heard someone walking behind me, when I was a body that
others followed.

A woman was shoved into a car at the shadowy mouth of a parking
garage, and the eyes that didn't know what they were witnessing at five
are the eyes I look through now.

The lessons are cumulative, the fear.

I must have known that being my own witness was itself a risk. How can
I see events unfolding when the body is completely symptomatic
of other bodies, including
its own.

The problem with memory is that only words can re-create it for others.

Each word its own past and desire
for a future.

Each word, each sentence, a fragment.

And how do you untangle from the telling the speaker's motives?

Isn't the second person a form of hiding? Why not just use the *I*?

My daughter said, hugging me, I am a barnacle and if you remove me
I will die.

It's taken me two decades to devise a good retort for each of the slights.
You'd be amazed at all the improvements in bathroom lighting, the ugly
remark before the mirror

diffused then clarified

the lover's words fading with the steam

to let the book appear.

A book ordered in prose and point of view. To witness my body as a
distant thing that gathers itself over time to become whole.

I wrote sentences that don't break. I sought narrative logic to order the
mess of memory.

At times I wanted to mistake myself for another and say, Sorry, you aren't
who I was looking for. Sorry to bother you.

The choices were not choices, the billboards were instructive and
censorious as I traveled to retrieve each self and found along the way
a daughter. I didn't use a map

and yet there she was in a heightened territory with my mother
and her mother before her

other mothers and other daughters.

I am weary but know now my fear is an accurate map, even if memory is
less than reliable.

And the lessons were never somewhere else, but in the hunch
of the shoulders before the screen of something I'd written and
erased a million times before.

The backspace would like me to tap out the soreness of the telling, until
the telling is gone and can move freely.

When I get to the ocean, I promise I'll submit a bikini top
that never did much for the soul.

For now, I leave my daughter this book as manual, as heirloom; like my mother's wedding dress in the unreachable part of my closet, both glamorous

and warning.

Would You?

1.

Would you carry your daughter on your back through a river? Would you ask someone to place her, knowing you will die, on the edge of a border highway? Would you lower her into the last boat that quickly fills like a ladle? Would she be pulled out and thrown like a fish into another country? Would you pray for a gentleness to buoy her when her bed capsizes under the weight of a stranger? Wait and wait for her, knowing she is dead? She is alive and all you have of her is a number written on your palm. Would you call and be transferred and put on hold? Every day? Would you hold hands as death comes over you? Her hand just the memory of her hand at seven? What would her hand look like now? Would you never forget it? Would she reach out to you every night, a picture she drew of you under her cot? Would you step into a rocking boat, its barely slats, its barely oars, and have her handed off to you like a heavy sack of tender fortunes? Would you yell at her to keep quiet? Cry when she isn't looking? Would you think, We'll die, we'll live, nothing can be done, we've sold off everything, everything's gone? Would you take a plane, a bus, a train? Walk and walk and dream of shade? Would you sing to her when she is too thirsty, too tired, too hungry? Would you turn on your tongue the name that keeps her from you and feel it clamp down like a thumbscrew?

2.

At the border checkpoint, the detention center behind her, a woman asks through a bullhorn, "How does it feel when you lose your child for a minute in the supermarket?" What if that minute turned into an hour, a year, a lifetime? Would you run crazy through the aisles, the streets, your head? Like the time you thought you left your daughter at the campsite under the West Texas sun, everyone else gone to the archaeology museum? How you imagined her at night, a lone wolf circling her, a pack of men? This is the second protest in four days. To get here, you had to walk down a long road, sheets of sand cutting diagonally into your faces. You forgot the sign your daughter made, a diptych of a mermaid submerged in the ocean singing, her arms, her hair waving above her freely. And next to her, the same mermaid—no musical notes orbiting her head, her hair limp—in a tiny cage. The sign could have shielded your daughter from the elements. How many more speeches, she wants to know, as an actor from your childhood is finally passed the bullhorn. You and her father take turns carrying her back to the car.

3.

You canoed on the river that morning. Your daughter in the front, you in the back, each paddling in contempt for the other, sending the canoe into the banks. You kept forgetting the guide's instructions: when heading into a giant rock, throw your body not forward but back. You cursed at her as you pushed the canoe off pebbly islets or out of mud with your paddle. "I'm doing all the work," you told her. "I'm too tired," she said. That night she begged to sleep in the tent with the other girls, and eager to be alone, to complete a thought, you let her go, to zip herself into its nylon walls. There the story was told of an angry father who murdered girls of about ten, and so she looked for you in the middle of the night and asked to be let back in. You fell asleep holding hands, and as the air mattress deflated, her body folded into yours. In the morning, when you kissed your daughter's humid brow, could you imagine it cold as a concrete floor?

4.

This is the protest for which you came, against yourself and your imagination. You want to yell through a bullhorn at your likeness, *Imagination is a privilege.* As is the supermarket. As is the air mattress. As is the canoe. And the tent. And your daughter's refusals and ennui. As is the paddle to push against the bank. As is the against, every shape carved out at the expense of someone else. As is the story told like a scary ride, that for a minute—as you raise your hands above your head and scream— liberates you from your body, its calcifications. As is the photo captured mid-ride that you decide not to buy. "Something happened to me when I was a little older than you," your mother told you at the end of the period talk. The imagination races, knees wound air as she climbs the hill to some unreachable safety. She was the girl the man was after. "I was able to get away, but I never told my mother." Not everyone exposed to the sun is working out a poem they'll later deem weak. Your mother once asked, "What does organic mean?" And before you could answer, she said, "Quiere decir mas caro, verdad?" It wasn't meant as a joke, but to preempt your virtue. You Earth-helper, you fair-trade checker, you poetry-soft center. She reminded your father every day to check his wallet for his green card before heading out the door. How they feared being hauled away for not speaking English, for looking like they didn't belong. Rounded up with all the Latin Americans they were quick to distinguish themselves from, even as they took in a friend and her son who were evading Immigration. Your father liked to tell the story of women, during the Spanish Civil War, whose heads were shaved and paraded down the street as warning. But that was another country, you wanted to say. You are going off course, you are so far from reason. You can hardly acknowledge that not all horrors lead to the family plot. This is the protest: You are here. You've been elsewhere and back. You can leave whenever you want. You have the passport to prove it. But you are grasping your daughter's thigh, bracing your body for the plane's impact. And who would you save if not her? In bed you read the news: the prisons and detention centers, the nursing homes, all filled with the dying, though what happens inside them is murky, the numbers rounded.

You, the Body & the Book

You lived with the body. There was no room for the book. You lived with the book, and the body broke a window trying to get in. You let the body stay the night on the couch and cleaned the cuts on its hands. The book said, I'm not jealous, but soon it begged for attention. At the poetry reading they both showed up and it was an impossible choice. In bed it was either the book or the body. At times zaftig, at times skinny. Neither of them looked better in the morning. You wiped their smudges after they got drunk and cried. Other books looked on smugly, cool and contained. They were all epiphany and apostrophe. The book made the body do impossible things, but only the body could bear another body and that was the question on the table. For a while you had very little to say to the book and worried the body was all you had.

You, the Bourgeoisie

The sensations were not, as they say, strange. It was a familiar tingling, like an army of ants that descends upon a static foot. Except this buzzing numbness moved across the oddest parts of your body, especially notice-able at work when there was nothing to do, when the assignment was to feign presence until the vacancy resolved. Unlike you in your twen-ties, the ants had a purpose. They'd march up the inner thighs into the vagina, then back down, or over the eyelids and lips, entering and exit-ing the sockets and mouth. With no health insurance, you took the bus to Planned Parenthood and tried to read the counselor's face as she ran her pen down your sexual history form. Or you asked your brother to hook you up with a doctor-client of his, who said, "Well, if it's all in your head, at least we know where it is." The more there was nothing to do, the more your symptoms led to endless worry rooms. You had trouble sleeping, and a friend at work said her boyfriend—who had left his wife and kids to unspring the trap Western culture had caught him in, who drained their savings to go East and return with a new name—could hover his hands over a body and release what was ailing it. And since your tiny apartment was already filled with bags of tree bark and dark bottles of oil and capsules, why not try one more thing when the paycheck cleared? He had a practice and placed you face-up on a massage table, where he scanned your body with his papery palms, stopping for several minutes at your neck as if magnetized to the area. People always asked about the pink-and-brown signature a surgeon had left when he took what hadn't been swallowed in childhood, so it wasn't surprising that from there a story would unfold. Which was this: during the French Revolution, a mob chased you into the street, held you down, and slit your throat. You were the bourgeoisie. They, the proletariat. That history—that rage, that vulnerability—is what you carry in your throat, he said. It will follow you from life to life. After the visit, you wondered whether being born this time into the working class was some type of karma, and how lucky to have had student health insurance when they found the thyroid cancer.

You & the Dying Languages

In the early and lonely days of mothering, when you felt old at forty-one, you'd examine pictures posted of homegrown arugula, read updates on a chicken coop's construction, the adoption of a baby goat. Everyone, it seemed, was washing cloth diapers, fermenting grains, ordering via poorly designed websites worms for their compost. They homeschooled, unschooled, free schooled, drove to the valley for a child-centered approach. Envying them, you rubbed lanolin on your nipples and declared it all a trend, like barbershop quartet mustaches or high-waisted jeans. You knew well the language of necessity and no way you'd speak it again. It was long gone with the factories and square of dirt between yard and shed, where your parents grew potatoes and lettuce and cucumbers, fertilizing them with chicken manure from a farm they'd drive to on weekends. Gone, too, the hens and rabbits, which you named and befriended before your mother swiftly snapped their necks. The pickling of vegetables, sewing of curtains, reupholstering the same terrible couch for years. Your father holding your brothers captive on weekends, only to botch after too many swigs one home improvement after another. Why hire a licensed contractor when your buddy from the factory has a concrete mixer to pave over the yard? Who needs a lawn anyway? Then there was the chorizo made with a grinder screwed to the kitchen table. You all wanted to crank it as your mother fed it chunks of meat. But only your father held the intestine to the funnel as it swelled and grew longer in his hands. Now you ask, were they really speaking the language of necessity or did you misunderstand the need—to make of a few recipes and the labor to produce them a way to lose no more than they had already lost, to speak in an endangered idiom to their kids, who would grow to be unlike them? Each meal a fraying tether to the homeland? If so, they couldn't just go to the A&P up the street. Everyone has their personal mythology, and for you it involves chicken liver and cow's brain. But in light of the peanut butter, in light of the reasonable hours and modest hungers, who are you? Only now and then do you yell across the house when you need something, flipping a switch that sheds light on your ignoble birth. Not long ago, you read an article about the generations of microbes dying out in the large intestine, thanks to the Big Macs broken down in the smaller one. How the researchers, a couple in California, diversified their microbial environment by fertilizing the kale in their garden with turkey manure, grinding their own wheat berries for pizza dough, even petting the family dog. And here you are, day after day, homogeneous microbes listless in yoga pants, unable to make much of anything, no skills to survive the apocalypse. You can't even make a simple A-line skirt for your daughter's American Girl doll (who survived, it should be noted, the 1918 flu inside a sooty tenement). You are hiding behind a hollow door, and when your daughter knocks you can't say, Leave me alone, I am making a poem, as if that's something useful. And it's not like you are saying it in Spanish; you gave up speaking it to her ages ago.

You & the Pendulum

She held a chain with a crystal suspended from it over different parts of your body and asked questions. Sometimes you told her what you needed to know, more often she dangled the pendulum over an organ to interrogate, implicitly, its proper functioning. These readings took place in her apartment, and although it was small and cluttered and had probably once been a cold-water flat, it must have been rent controlled because how else could she live there, in that inflated market. At thirty, you were having stomach issues, like you did as a child, and she demonstrated how to massage the intestine, advising, based on the pendulum's answers, to stay away from most nightshades. She sought a second opinion by holding the pendulum over the tomatoes on her kitchen table. This seemed more efficient and less frightening than a million needles pushed into the skin. But the question you waited to ask until the end was about the scientist with the British accent. Your gut told you it would end with the summer, but as she held the pendulum and asked if he was your future, the chain began to vibrate and then turn, swinging the crystal in increasingly wider circles, faster and faster in the direction of yes. You wrote her a check and headed for a pay phone to tell your scientist about the diagnosis.

You to the Future

What would you have said to the future? Future, you will have no scientist in it. Future, your scientist was kissing a Canadian. Future, you could have told me, "Don't go to his apartment, depress the doorbell for many seconds, wait around the corner in his favorite diner, call him from the dark and humid underground of your last rumbling hope." But, Future, let me tell you something truly remarkable: there were pay phones on subway platforms, which was great when you needed one, but if you needed one, things were often not so great. You were late for an interview, or you wanted to be told, "Don't get on that train. I love you. Come back to bed." No one on a subway pay phone wanted to hear, "Hold on." You were lost, trying to buy weed, calling some guy's beeper. The receiver and keypad were archives of body-cum-city, and in these moments of disorientation, of numbers black and waxy and sticky, the pointer finger brought you closer to your desire with its impeccable memory. You needn't be told lovers will misfire feelings wherever and whatever the mode, but in you, Future, no one will know what it's like to make a collect call, to reverse the charges. Nor remember the ode a Spanish poet wrote to his light bulb late one night in the kitchen.

You, Supplicant

Over sashimi tostadas and chelas, you tell your girlfriends about the time you kneeled on the carpeted stairs that led to the bedroom of the guy who dumped you, pleading. O, his long hair—his thinness—like Jesus! They said they couldn't see it. "You, for a man, begging?" And how his roommate gently lifted you to your feet, an act of kindness like so many meted out in those days by men adjacent to another man's destruction. He was trying to pull you from the image of yourself, not as beautiful but as a supplicant before beauty. A penitent whose suffering was the deep and persistent condition of being a woman. It was, like dictatorship, like First Communion, a perversion. You didn't say this to your girlfriends. You moved on to translation problems, and your humiliations remained fuzzy backdrops, like bookcases in author photos.

What Does Your Daughter Wish For?

At the vigil, your daughter and her friend throw pennies into the fountain, then run back to you, screaming for more. Embarrassed by their joy while others are suffering, you tell them to be quiet, to think of the dead. They bow their heads for several seconds and try not to giggle. Their childhood of protests, of battery-powered candles. What do they wish for as their investments disappear under murky water? Animatronic creatures that rise magnificently into the air before crashing into the curtains? That's for babies, they'd say. You can't keep up with children's desires or how the market shapes them. In the coming months, there will be more protests, more vigils, and when one fad dies, TikTok will give another life. Someone tweets: now that everyone is remote learning, the air is cleaner, and empty classrooms means no children for a crazed shooter to target. But you are sure, because you've read the history of fathers, that violence has only been pulled further inward, fortified inside the home, where it has always been and where it began, training upon its first objects, testing its range. You think of childhood, that Summer of Sam, the mushroom cloud on the cover of *Time*. A hurricane at the Jersey shore you thought would reach your bed. How the waves of worry came and went and came and went, and yet you played pretend like your daughter, like her friend, who across a screen are making hospital gowns and masks for their dolls. You ask her if she's sad or scared of getting sick. "No," she says, "I'm just bored." "Can we watch *Stranger Things*?"

Your Daughter Refashions the Flag into a Crop Top

The frayed flag of a disputed territory that barely covered your sex: the thing woven onto you, the thing you had to accept. Yoko Ono put on a stage how you knelt and kept quiet, as small, buffoonish men snipped and snipped. You even provided the dull scissors. In Cecilia Vicuña's painting *Amaranta,* there are a thousand invisible folds of what happened before and after. Though the original painting and your mother no longer exist, they've put in a long-distance call to your daughter, who has begun to hear footfalls behind her as she walks around the block. Cecilia once thought she had to choose between poetry and painting, but she no longer believes this and is recovering what was lost, rejected, stolen. To your daughter you bequeath what was left of the flag, and rejecting its unflattering form, she refashions it into a crop top to show off her midriff. She's on the verge of something, that beautiful precipice. On Zoom, her teacher greets the class cheerily before sharing his screen. But instead of a lesson, he opens the picture of a woman he keeps on his desktop, undressed. "Awkward!" your daughter writes to her friend in the chat, and though they laugh it off, you know he's gotten into their heads. "Hombres necios," like bleeding, you are done with them.

You Rode a Loop

From your house on the corner to the factory at the end of the street, then back again: this was the loop your mother let you ride, not along the avenue with its cavalcade of trucks, or up the block where Drac the Dropout waited to plunge his pointy incisors into virgin necks. You can't remember exactly your age, but you probably had a bike with a banana seat, and wore cutoff jeans and sweat socks to the knees. You are trying to be precise, but everything is a carbon-like surface that scrolls by with pinpricks emitting memory's wavy threads. One is blindingly bright and lasts only seconds: you are riding your bike, and the shadowy blots behind the factory windows' steel grates emit sounds that reach and wrap around you like a type of gravity that pulls down the face. You can't see them but what they say is what men say all day long to women trying to get somewhere. It's not something you hadn't heard before, but until then, you'd only had your ass grabbed by boys your age—boys you knew, boys you could name—in a daily playground game in which teachers looked away. In another pinprick, you loop back to your house, where your mother is standing on the corner talking to neighbors. You tell her what the men said and ask, "Does this mean I'm beautiful?" What did she say? Try remembering: you are standing on the corner with your mother. You are standing on the corner. This pinprick emits no light; it is dark, it is her silence. Someday you will have a daughter, and the dead-end street will become a cul-de-sac, and all the factories will be shut down or across the border, and the men behind screens will be monitored, blocked. When things seem safe and everything is green and historic and homey, you will let her walk from school to park, where you'll wait for her, thanks to a flexible schedule, on the corner. And when she daydreams along the way, taking too long to reach you, the words they said will crawl through the tree you wait under.

You Lie

When you asked your brother how many lies would land you in hell, he said, One hundred. A good, round number: high enough to impress a child just learning to count, infinite in its achievable terror. So, you kept count and lost count and started over. Until that day on the way home from school, when you didn't bother with the crosswalk and walked diagonally across the street, toward the empty lot where poison sumac trespassed its fence, and asked no one: What about the everyday lies you were under contract to manufacture, that you didn't tally because they were shared with your mother and father? Were those exempt from God's punishment? Like the time you found a wallet in the cafeteria with five bucks in it, and they said: Turn it in? Don't be stupid. When the union rep was at the door with your father's disability check, or you answered the phone and it was the Avon lady. You knew to play innocent and nail your line: Sorry, they're not home. Lo siento. No one needs to know your father's sleeping it off. Your mother can't rely on overtime. That your dress, pretty as it is, is a Goodwill find. The street was thin with cars minutes before the factories let out. And how you suspected the poison sumac was just some kind of weed and harmless, but who would touch it to prove otherwise? Everything was lies, and there was nothing to keep you from your own fabrications, no eternal fire. A little lie might make you interesting. Help you fit in. Even now, you wonder if Rosalba's father was really a jukebox repairman. You all watched *Sha Na Na* and *Happy Days* and wanted to believe it. To believe a father so intimate with the glorified American past, when no father you knew had whiled away his youth sipping root beer floats at the soda shop. No mother had sock-hopped in a poodle skirt. That's why you wore that past as a Halloween costume. Oh, shit, here comes Papa walking into this poem. He's going to kick your ass for not coming straight home.

You, Escape Artist

The night she told you, you dreamt he stood in the room watching you sleep next to her. What she had locked in her diary became a key to dark foyers, held beneath the tongue. One mother said it never happened; the other, no more sleepovers. Why should another be sacrificed, you ask your therapist, and not you? Why didn't he mistake your body for hers? You no longer hold the key but the impression it left. After another near-miss, you slept for weeks with the light on and threw off the covers to find nothing there except the shadow you call Could-Have-Been-Worse. Is a shadow worth a story? If not, how to cast it off? Your daughter has just learned about Houdini, how he escaped from a milk can submerged in water, and she begs you all evening to tie her up beneath her desk and time her as she loosens the red rope from her ankles and wrists. She wants increasingly elaborate configurations and to beat her own record. What are you preparing her for? When you pour a cup of water over her head and say, your body is yours—meaning hers? Houdini practiced for hours all his techniques, which weren't just tricks, your daughter insists, but the ability to hold his breath for several minutes or tighten his stomach to take any blow. Yet nothing could have prepared him for the brute who'd slip into his dressing room and, without warning, punch the air out of him. Houdini went on to perform that night and, ignoring the pain for days, die in bed of a burst appendix. Eventually she gets bored of the game and wants a snack, and you try to tell her you'll always undo the knots if she gets trapped, and she says, Okay, Mama, okay. Tell me the story of the girl who can't stop vomiting.

What Did You Dream?

In your white gown with the crocheted bodice, you entered that summer night the interior garden. Thirst led you to the terra-cotta jug in the corner, to lift the waxed lace from its spout and tilt it above you until a clear arc of water, cool as the clay that contained it, poured into the well of your mouth. You stood in that verdant enclosure, feet on glazed tile conduits to sky, river, ocean, and listened to the sleep sounds of those you loved seep through the shutters. Moon outlined your perfect body behind scrim of linen; you were the virgin commemorating her own death, dove alit on each hand, one held lightly to the lips. You returned to bed, and what did you dream? A scorpion waiting in a slipper? Or the time she told of the poison that slips in at night, how no one believed her?

Your Mother's Advice

Run into a school if a man is chasing you. Run into a church. Fall in love with art and mess up your dress. Dream all you want but baste before you sew. Ring someone's doorbell, ask to use their phone. Priests are men too. Better yet, stay home. If you skimp, you soak. If you boil, skim the foam. In love, as in war, every hole is a trench. Devil you know, or end up alone. Even the prettiest mole can sprout a whisker. Dime con quién andas and I'll tell you who you are. Run into a store. Shop until you're safe. Run into a hospital, any public place. Do not take rides. Do not lead him to your car or door. Key him in the eye, knee him in the balls. Do not tell your brothers, they'll kill him. If you must, tell the killer you love him. Then run toward headlights, never the woods. A man will say he loves you to keep you from books. Tell a nurse. Dissimulate. Have the sense not to get caught shoplifting. Keep your mouth shut when you laugh. Keep your business off the curb. It's all in the sofrito (just watch & learn). Do not tell your friend her fiancé tried to kiss you as you slept on their couch after the engagement party. Everyone will blame you. They'll call you mosquita muerta. They'll call you fake. Keep a plant on your desk, straighten up before you leave. A good dancer isn't always the best husband. Dispose properly of sanitary napkins. Steer clear of white jeans. Get pregnant and your father will kill you. Never say no to a party, las malas lenguas can wag all they want when the music's over.

What You Knew About Virginity

That it was something to be given in holy matrimony. That it was the only thing you had to give. That once you handed it over, you could never get it back. That it was a tightly woven hammock rocking an idea inside you. That a piercing pain meant both hammock and idea gone. That in flamenco songs, women exited the bride's chamber triumphantly waving a handkerchief bloomed with blood. That blood was the signature on a rare document. That other ideas would replace or join the first in the calculus of saving yourself or giving it up: slut, whore, nympho, easy—or else, goody-two-shoes, stuck up, cocktease. Lousy, like Sandy, with virginity. Ideas that were not yours but who you'd, nevertheless, be. Not long ago, you ran into a friend who worked with the guy you dated freshman year. The senior who dropped you off a street over so your father wouldn't know. The artist, the Chilean. The one who cost you a friend because she liked him first. The shiny black hair and pink leather tie. The boyfriend who ghosted you before that had a name. "How's he doing," you asked your friend, and then, "Why did he stop calling?" Somehow it still mattered after so many years. "Because you didn't put out," she relayed. That sex was something to put out, like the cat, like the trash, like a fire. That there is a Cult of the Black Virgin in Europe and that your mother, who worshipped La Virgen de Montserrat for healing her son, would always prefer your blondest of boyfriends. That people waited for hours to touch the gold orb resting on her palm and be blessed by baby Jesus on her lap. Despite many theories regarding the origins of these Madonnas, one thing was certain: above all, be a virgin and give birth to a savior, and you will be placed deep in a mountain, a shrine for seekers, penitents, or the simply curious. Take great care in who receives this precious gift, which you had no part in choosing. That sometimes you lost it before you could give it: there were horses and bikes, swings and seesaws, on which pleasure collided with injury. That inside those horses were sometimes men in armor, offering the spoils of war, or else endless popcorn shrimp, Spanish fly, or pity. Beneath the armor, men like a stepfather or a teacher or a neighbor. In that case, as in all pillaging, what you had to offer was taken. The gift gone, your entire useless self would become the thing no one wanted. Labeled damaged goods. That damaged goods could go on to have an okay life, but your husband would always know he got second prize. Even if hubby wasn't much of a prize, you only had yourself to blame. That certain things were loopholes to pleasure: rubbing up against a best friend, for example. Or in the froth of make-out sessions with your boyfriend, doing everything but. To cross the magical border, you had to hold hands with your one true love, then fall back onto a white bed covered in rose petals. That Hymen—okay, you didn't know this then—was a god and also a genre of lyric poetry. That Hymen was invited to every wedding but never took a plus-one. That Hymen was Bacchus and Aphrodite's son, which must have made him seem a little uptight next to his parents. Other things you did not know then: that all hymens, like snowflakes, are different. That some are born without hymens. That some have super-duper bulletproof hymens, which can be a real problem. Hymens can't grow back, as you once believed, but surgery can restore them. Having looked at pictures of hymens (for research!), you'd prefer yours not sewn back to its original state but replaced with a bedazzled prosthesis that stands out from the surrounding meat. Why would anyone care about having, or not, a hymen in this day and age, but there you have it. You've heard about vaginal and labial rejuvenation, so maybe it's all part of the same shitty erasure poem to which a woman's life is subjected. Can you wave a wand and pretend this or that was never said, never happened? The baby that pushed its cannonball-sized head through you? The loser boyfriend? The frat party? Any sleepless night in which you cried? You lost your virginity during a study abroad, to a boy both blond and cruel. Lost is a strange way to describe it because you know exactly where and when you left it. It didn't hurt or sting. You didn't bleed. You felt, in fact, just as you did before you hailed a cab at 3 a.m., meaning a little confused and a little lonely. But it could have been the beer, the foreign country.

You, Glistening in the Meadow

When were you taught a woman's body is a trap that chews through the foot of a decent man on his way to good deeds? To his mother's house, where something always needs fixing? How did you learn to sharpen the teeth and test the spring before hiding in a tuft of grass? The dog's slobber wets your metal as he vaults easily over, and there, glistening in the meadow, you wait to hear the happy whistle of its owner. They'll say, That day, he didn't return with a beautiful partridge in his leather satchel but with one less foot. And somewhere, a woman's body, a trap, wears it proudly like an amulet.

You & the Rapper

He led you, your bike behind his, to the plastics factory on the edge of the neighborhood. He was going to impart a lesson on French-kissing, which in your neighborhood was called *rapping*. But rapping wasn't talking, as in the old parlance, because there was another tongue in your mouth. Were those expressions—like *truck* for souped-up bike—simply imagined? There are no entries for them on Urban Dictionary. That you still say them is no more proof of their existence than whimsical watercolor renderings of Atlantis. What happened next is that he pressed you against the loading dock and came at you open-mouthed, his tongue boring into you like a bit from your father's toolbox. So you just let yourself be bored and tried to follow along, until he grabbed your head in his hands and said, "Stop moving." You hovered your lids half-open to watch him kiss you, to see how it was done, and staring back were his eyeballs bulging from their sockets like a horny toad's. Even then you understood that in kissing, closing the eyes was de rigueur. Afraid you'd laugh inside his mouth, you unhooked your hands from his shoulders and wriggled out of the enclosure, and without learning the mechanics of rapping, rode off on your truck to tell your friends, the threads of your cutoffs throbbing against your thighs as you pumped up the hill.

While Your Fathers Did Second Shifts

Because your fathers fled a dictatorship only to set up their own, and took with them the belief that a woman shouldn't enter a bar unless it was an emergency and had to use the pay phone, you shared with your cousins one eyeliner pencil, applying in rearview mirrors the blackest breves to lower lids. And you know what thick kohl along the waterline leads to? The island of Spanish fathers' nightmares, so close you could reach it in your hormone-powered boat. Where in dark basements, you waved accents in the air with boys from Puerto Rico, the DR, and let them click their hip bones into yours. Until someone's mother came down and flipped the lights on and threw everyone out. O, América, opening beyond the ocean of a father's vigilance as he does a second shift! Nothing could have kept you from what you'd become. Not even the pink eye, which Mamá treated with té de manzanilla compresses.

You, Amateur Interpreter

You would have told yourself as your mother sat in the dentist's chair, had you known who Wittgenstein was then, "I have to imagine pain which I *don't feel* on the model of pain which I *do feel*." You would have considered whether deep nerve pain was more akin to an arm scraping against pavement or to the head struck by a slipper flung from across a room just after breakfast. But that wouldn't have solved the problem of translation: first, build the model, then describe its components in another language so that the model falls apart and becomes another. Meaning, could you have described your mother's pain to the doctor in English, even if you felt it in your own jaw? You'd watched your Mamá's teeth being pulled or a mold made of her mouth. Dentures have to fit perfectly or they hurt. You did your best, telling her to bite down hard into the wax. Did your parents ever have a full set of teeth? When you had yours pulled—the wisdom and the one dead at the root—there was nothing to interpret but the ether. So you lay back in leather and let the dentist, like a lover, blow smoke into your mouth until the chair began to swirl—a tipsy teacup at the church bazaar—and whip your hair around. Later, you got a well-paid gig at Avon's international awards dinner and sat with the top Latin American sellers, and, oh god, you were hungry and didn't have half the words for the cosmetic industry. But the agency never bothered to ask, so you faked it and brought home leftovers. Those ladies deserved better than your parent-teacher conference training. Anyone in the kitchen could have done a better job. In high school, when you tried to test out of Spanish and were asked to spell out numbers, you thought, qué fácil, but ended up in the same group as the metal chicks from the suburbs. When you were a baby, Papá's first English swung into the back of the restaurant with each stack of dishes, and with a box of diapers under each arm, he'd come home singing, "Happy Birthday, para mí. Happy Birthday, para mí."

Tu Mamá

Gave birth to her own translator. How's that for the afterlife of the original?

How You Became a Poet

The day your father slammed the door shut as your mother was trying to leave. The day he struck her face. The click of the bolt. No archive to prove it, except your body tensioning at the sound of a dish thrown too loudly into the sink. There were two windows with short curtains. A doll in a crocheted dress peering from a corner shelf, her arms outstretched. A radio kept on all day. The black hair on your father's sinewy arm, the rolled-up sleeve. Memory's overreliance on synecdoche. You want to make out the figure of your whole tiny body at three, in the kitchen, witnessing. You were learning not that a woman can't move up but that she can't get out. What would they have done if they knew their daughter was recording in the chest and in the breath the rhythm of their unhappiness? You were invisible but with such big eyes. In time, your father did worry that the unlettered child would one day side with English and rat out the immigrants that were her parents. The more he drank the more his kids became spies. What you can offer in their defense is a rhyme scheme, like a pretty braid, that says: "Yes, bless them, they did their best / They were model permanent residents."

A Girl Like You

if ever I see you again
as I have sought you
daily without success

I'll speak to you, alas
too late! ask,
What are you doing on the

streets of Paterson?

—WILLIAM CARLOS WILLIAMS, FROM *PATERSON*

1.

You made it into the lobby in the usual fashion. With a high school education, you answered an ad in the newspaper, probably the type for reception: eighteen, a little plump, pretty. Bilingual but not *too* bilingual. You held the line for the publisher, who saw in you something special. So you walked your white pumps into the newsroom, as in a Hollywood biopic, and shoved press release after press release into dozens of slots. Later, a step up: on weekends, you wrote obits, mainly of war veterans, and were on friendly terms with all the funeral directors. One day the deceased wasn't a member of the Knights of Columbus, married to his high school sweetheart (*née* something). She was a girl, surname kept private, whose tender body was discovered next to the Cuban bodega where your mother would send you for bread. She was thirteen. You, a college freshman. When you told the city desk you were from that place and spoke its language, they said stop sorting and ride with the reporter to the scene. What were you thinking among your neighbors, flipping your skinny notebook as you translated what they said? Did you feel like an anthropologist among your own? You can still feel the excitement in the newsroom as the deadline loomed, the booming voice of the editor, his Texas drawl. How he asked for a first-person account of growing up in the neighborhood to accompany the story, and you wrote that although you avoided the street where she was found, you were never afraid. A kiss blown is no blow to the head. You must have felt important, suddenly someone to the reporters, the editors, who flirted and wondered aloud if you could jimmy a lock. Just like that, your name, a syllable less then, appeared on the newspaper's front page. You didn't know it yet, but you'd spend the rest of your life mapping the difference between the girl in the newsroom and the girl in the news.

2. (A Girl Like You Talks Back)

I know you've never stopped thinking about me, how similar we were except in how we got out of the neighborhood. My mother also sent me to the bodega, but instead for a bag of rice. I lived in the same apartment building as you once had. I learned to just keep walking past men who thought they were encouraging my budding body, but sometimes I'd talk back, some part of me always ready to fight. I had crushes on boys who wanted to be like their older brothers, their baby faces in front of the candy store pretending to be drug dealers. What they did with my body they did for the last time. They took me, all of them; he who did it and those who said nothing. I was beginning to understand the body I was becoming, what it said to them and seemed to invite. My silence was also my body. How my head hung, how I walked quickly, how I didn't look at them. You wrote many years ago that until they found me, you felt safe, but still, you avoided the street where men gathered and read back to you your own body, that of your cousins. How little you understood safety then, even when I learned for you its limits. Now you are fifty, and I'm still thirteen. Both of our mothers are buried, mine next to me, and for eternity I'll have to assure her it wasn't her fault. The men who approach us now speak softly, gently. They even leave flowers. You are trying to find me on the internet, to know more of me than my brutal end. Googling me, you learn of another girl with the same name, who a few towns over suffered the same fate at the hands of a neighbor. But there will always be another girl with the same name, in the same state. I know that's not what you want. You want to know who did it, how it could have happened to me and not you. You want to weave the answer into a cross to protect the door to your daughter's room. Or worse, for a poem. I am always of some use, of course. At your service. What? You thought you'd conjure me, and I'd answer your questions, eager to have my words in print, like those neighbors who crowded around you? Your mother ran from a man she never named, and taught you to do the same. She never said you could change the world, only that you should run. And what keeps you up at night is that I couldn't run fast enough, and that if a girl trips as she flees, her story ends abruptly. It doesn't click shut like a well-made poem, but with a thud like the lid of a dumpster. It should be evident to all your readers that you are speaking, not me. That you prop up the dead for your own purposes. Was your first intention to make my murder *elegiac*? Remember when you couldn't pronounce that word correctly, when others saw you as you were, a girl who knew so little but elbowed herself to the front to be heard?

You in Cutoffs

You were maybe at your skinniest then. You wore cutoff jeans, Pumas, and a faux football jersey so tight your friends laughed and called you Jugs when you wore it. You hated football or didn't care, and had yet to fall in love with a musician or become the crying girl who'd call in the middle of the night looking for him. It was the summer to be cool and light, to be lifted and carried across bodies until the bouncer had to pluck you from the lip of the stage and send you down the stairs. You'd make it back to the center and signal skyward with your thumb, and someone would let you step into their interlaced fingers to boost you up. The bouncer looked annoyed each time you landed at his feet, but you could tell he really wasn't; you were small and cute and easy to pass from hand to hand.

You, a Hand, Another

The following summer, you went to another concert and gave the thumbs-up, and as you were carried, felt a hand inside your cutoffs and another under your shirt. Then another hand and another, as if the only thing keeping you up were also trying to crawl inside you. You started to kick back and punch down at anyone below, even though it meant that hands, innocent or not, could pull away from your body, withdraw their support, let you drop. The one you loved—who thought crying girls a continuum—begged you in a letter not to risk yourself on a roof of strange fingers, and told the cautionary tale of a friend who fell into a sea of glass and with tweezers had to pick each green and brown shard from his arms and legs. By then, he was no longer a boyfriend, just a pen pal who liked to sound wise somewhere out West. But you never fell, you made it out of the crowd and back to the tent, where friends told similar stories. "Fuck those motherfuckers," the toughest girl said, "nothing's going to keep me from going back in."

You in Palazzo Pants

> Íbamos a escribir nuestros más bellos poemas robando
> tiempo a las horas de oficina.
>
> —SARA URIBE

He agreed to meet in one of those cafés you would write in if you could afford that city. He was also a writer, but older, and you wanted to know how to get published. "Slip a picture of yourself in with your poems," he advised, as in toss your shiny coin into the fountain—heads or tails— before it tarnishes. You didn't tell him of the internship you once had, in which the only thing that stood between the slush pile and the top editor was you in palazzo pants. That the top editor was a tall, ash-blonde woman who thought your Post-it notes on manuscripts clever. You didn't tell him this because you have only thought of it now. At the time, you probably flirted like a knee that responds to a little hammer. When you told a therapist about the hand that slid down your back as you fixed sentences, she asked, "Well, were you at least flattered?" In both cases, yes. But like a bouquet of flowers, what do you say when it arrives on your desk without a card? The other secretaries expect you to be excited. They hover around your desk, clucking: We never get anything, we're so jealous. Still, the water will soon turn murky, and the flowers stink, and you are left with the burden of taking the whole thing out of the building. Now when you imagine your own poems arriving with a picture of yourself back then, you want to write a note in curvy pink, tell them how beautiful they are, how worthy of an audience.

You & the Bosses

The boss who emails a poem he wrote, in which "the speaker" fucks his wife. What do you think, he wants to know? That he's trying to impress with his diction's stamina, how it bulges and strains toward the epiphany. But you take pity and suggest he break it into stanzas. The one who boasts, when you slide away from him in the booth, that he has all the lovers he needs. He's so good in the sack they cry out, "Take me home!" Which reminds me, you say, it's time to go. In every classroom and in every book, the well-meaning bosses who decree no adverbs, no exclamation points, no foreign language, but especially no sincerity. Obedient at work, you come home and kick your poems for seeming too needy, too amateurish. You only have yourself to blame for these failures: you forget to take minutes, arrive late, bustier under blazer. The boss who picks up a lemon from the bar and says his balls are like *this* and squeezes hard. Twenty years hence, you still have no idea what he meant. The lady boss inside you who knows not to cry or show mercy. Your daughter points to an entry in her dream dictionary: "A man can expect great wealth and prestige if his dream features a diploma. For a woman, however, this dream warns of problems resulting from hubris." "That's sexism. Right, Mama?"

Not, "What Can You Remember?"

> A man like a city and a woman like a flower
> —who are in love. Two women. Three women.
> Innumerable women, each like a flower.
>
> —WILLIAM CARLOS WILLIAMS, FROM *PATERSON*

What can you not forget? You had a yeast infection. You weren't in the mood, that old euphemism. You went with your boyfriend, the Deadhead, to the Paterson Falls, near where you lived. It was a warm night, you wore a wrap skirt, your hair loose. You were in your braless phase. A man appeared from behind a tree and asked your boyfriend for a cigarette. You'll never forget the camaraderie between them, their ease. How your boyfriend, long-limbed and loose, reached for his Bic, and the stranger curled his body over it and cupped the flame. A ritual greeting between two men. Wanting to seem cool, tough, unafraid, you smiled at the man as he disappeared again behind the tree. When you say you fear nature, you mean your own instinct. To tell this story, you'll need some caffeine. A Coke? Nope. A double espresso. If anyone had been in the park that night, would it have seemed a scuffle between two boys for a girl's attention? How could it have happened with your boyfriend there next to you, ask the well-intentioned. You have no answer, except their fingers were indistinguishable in the dark recesses of your body. Minutes later, the boyfriend put forth, in defense of the stranger, an insanity plea: "You know, I think he's just crazy." Have you seen that movie with the unconventionally handsome bus driver who is also a poet? In one scene, he is a flaneur ambling to work, past the Falls and the old silk mills turned artist housing. The lens widens and renders it all pastoral; he is thinking. Had a woman been the lead, immediately a car would have slowed as she walked faster, the driver leaning out the window to ask, "Aww, what's wrong? Give me a smile." But the poet-slash-bus-driver continues unbothered and stops to talk to a girl sitting alone in front of a former factory, writing in her journal. Had you written the script, she'd be gone the moment he asks her to read him a poem. What is the fantasy, you'd like to know? "Poetry is great emotion recollected in tranquility." You gathered from your shirt the hair yanked from your head and threw it out the window as you drove past a cop car. Your mother mended your beloved Gap shirt. You blamed it on volleyball.

You Are Officially in Menopause

when for a full year you don't

read Williams. There's no going back

you think, but one morning

find yourself reading

Journey to Love—

a terrible title.

#NotAllHands

I was not even / afraid of your hand, / only
sometimes, and too late.

—INGEBORG BACHMANN

Mostly the hands smoothed the hair when they landed on the head. They
pressed lightly the arm or palm. When they raised up it was usually to
wave. If they approached the face, nine times out of ten it was to cup the
cheek. Unbidden, they gave pleasure and placed trash bins at the curb.
One hand opened the door, the other shut a window to the storm. But
what of the other hands, the other times not spoken? Any gesture can
cause a flinch. Pleasure turn sleight of hand. You know that exam the
optometrist gives, with lines that wiggle at the edges of the screen, and
how you are instructed to click each time they are perceived? How they
keep moving from one place to another, causing you to question whether
it's the afterimage or the real thing? You're sure you'll fail the test, eye-
balls vibrating, eyeballs shifting, body one big eyeball, like that draw-
ing in an essay by Emerson. There are hands that move thus in memory's
periphery. But by the knuckles, can a man be identified? His intentions
known? All you can do is keep your face pressed into the viewfinder.
Click. Click. Click. Click. Click.

You Were an Asshole

Not a victim. You pocketed the twenty he pushed across the table as you poured olive oil into his bowl. You knew exactly what you were doing, you did it purposefully. You did it slow. You slipped boyfriends up your sleeve as if cheap rings, and when they fell out, you said you were holding them for a friend. You dropped off the sweetest of them at the station a day earlier than planned, thinking yourself smarter than him. And you may have been. But you could have waited with him for the train to come. On Valentine's Day, you half-heartedly visited your father, and he died the next morning. You never stole money, or from anyone's house, but you used the boss's FedEx account to send manuscripts to contests you'd never win. Pretending to know things you didn't know, you got through school and the job you have now. You never returned that book "the American housewife has been waiting for." Instead, you smoked and drank and talked shit. The library in the old neighborhood has been shuttered forever. Otherwise, the fines would be enormous.

You Were No Saint

> Saint Lucy is said to have gouged out her eyes when a suitor admired them; Saint Catherine of Siena sheared off her beautiful long hair. Saint Teresa was more moderate, but she did shoot down a gentleman who admired her shapely foot by telling him "take a good look—this is the last time you'll ever see it."
>
> —CATHLEEN MEDWICK, *TERESA OF AVILA: THE PROGRESS OF A SOUL*

You were never one to pull your foot into the darkness of the tunic's folds. Show it all off, the long curly hair, a very short skirt. That was your motto. Is there a way to be that involves sneakers and a clean face? Who would want to carry their eyes in a bowl, anyway? Yet, the years come like velvet curtains over dazzling bodies, stuck now with failing sight, failing to be seen.

You: Promo

Whose ear could cut through any accent like butter? Who could type while orchestrating an orgy? Who, said the agency, would go straight to the top with a good blowout? Who walked through the rain listening to Chaka Khan? Who could keep an evening look hidden under a suit like a smoking habit? Who would jump over turnstiles in platform boots if she heard the train coming? Who named a famous actor's baby? Who could dance herself thin in all musical categories? Who did the lead singer mistake for A&R? Who shrugged when he left and slept with the drummer? Who remembers the Copacabana like it was a movie, with a Cuban finally cast as a Cuban? Who said on her break, hey aren't you Plácido Domingo? And to whom did the tenor say, Why yes, and who are you, in fairytale Castilian? A fur collar, a newsboy cap, a pair of overplucked eyebrows. That's who.

You & the Banker

He was twice divorced, a history buff, and fond, he said eyeing the skinny blonde behind you, of the ethnic type. As you ate each petit course, almost as a filmic joke, you made a note to get falafel from your favorite street vendor on the way home. Instead, you let him take you to an antique shop, up narrow, squeaky stairs, to buy an engraving sliced from a rare book. He needed art for his summer home with the ocean view. You felt sick for wanting that life: ships that could sail so out of context. Or, he said, what about this whale?

When Did You Become Your Mother?

Your mother is wearing your skin, pulling the thread out of your mouth and through the eye of the needle. It is your foot in it its own shoe she presses to the machine's peddle, and from shoulder to hand, she maneuvers you to leave her steady signature in stitch after un-jumped stitch. You sense her mainly when performing domestic tasks, when you stop reading about abjection long enough to scrub the oven and ask (knowing all your cleansers are organic): "Where is the can of Comet?" With an expertise for making beds you never acquired, her hand inside yours tucks the bedspread under the lip of the pillow on which you cried yourself to sleep. Your palm smashes garlic to loosen its skin, and the thwack is hers, maybe also her anger. Body that couldn't comfort returns in a long glug of oil and two bay leaves. O, hand that feels the inside of the pot for assurance. To know it's been properly washed, she'd say, the eyes can't be trusted, just the pads of the fingers. Although you look nothing like her, some say she's in the gestures, in the features only others can see. But it's in the way you clean and hold a grudge. When years ago, in a taxi with someone you met at a bar, when the entire ride he slipped "A little bit of Rosa" into "Mambo No. 5." When you didn't know where the taxi was going, everything so slow and so blurry. Was that your mother's hand fumbling too long for the keys, stalling his entry? They say women become their mothers at thirty-one, your age then, but you fought the thought of her and opened a window to let in noise of cars and revelers below. What you didn't know is that even alive she was a ghost, and that night manifested herself in your kitchen, waiting for you to wake up, to come to your senses. Why couldn't you hear her when she said, "Would you like an omelet?" You feel her now when hot oil jumps from pan to skin.

You & the Donkey Cart

You had in your cart a disease that needed pulling. You had a musical of drunk uncles that slept piled on each other all morning. In your cart, a crate of Dollar Store epiphanies that kept slipping through the slats. A few did and set up shop. You had a work ethic and an American Dream, because someone said they were yours and you could keep them. Buried beneath were seaweed and sand from the shores of an arrival. Also, a torn sail and oranges, por si las moscas. You had girlhood, its peel-off polish. And your tiny mother, recovered from the railroad tracks where she was miming a silent movie among the dope addicts. But with no donkey to beat forward with a stick, you pulled the cart to gatherings found in the calendar of events and did a little jig, which they took for flamenco. You found yourself a poet, a painter, who flexed their concepts but were too lazy to carry the load. Never did they offer so much as an ode or portrait as compensation for the ride. Though you got to the next town and the next, you never thought to dump the cart's contents and walk, your body the only burden.

You Decide at Fifty to Finally Become Elegant

> You haven't even begun. You must pause first,
> the way one must always pause before a great spirit,
> if only to take a good breath.
>
> —MARY RUEFLE

You'd control both fringe and frizz, and whittle your wardrobe down to ten timeless, interchangeable pieces in monochromatic black, white, and gray. No longer would you be lured by the designer dress sold "as is" or whatever trend worn by students who stare blankly when you mention Grace Jones. So far, you've acquired an impeccably tailored blazer in a kill-two-birds with one houndstooth print. On the floor of the closet, two boxes: One labeled, *Who Do You Think You Are?* The other, *It Itches.* They remain empty as you scroll endlessly for old-money effortlessness. Last night your eyes throbbed from staring too long at a screen, and feeling a headache coming on, you canceled the mani-pedi for the next day. Then, as if your brain were desperate to wriggle out of the Spanx of your narrow focus, a dream enveloped you in a flowy caftan of every imaginable print and color, like those the sex-starved Mrs. Roper wore on *Three's Company.* The caftan was hundreds of individual pieces of fabric that levitated over your body, and to it you added more and more accessories, confident in your taste and allure. Earrings hit your shoulders, your hair postcoital. But then a long-lost ex entered the dressing room through the mirror and told you the scarf covered in red and pink flowers was pushing it. You took off the scarf to please him, and woke from the dream in your faded pajamas, next to the man who rarely notices. Was the dream an allergic reaction to class aspiration? Set off by regret and hormones? The caftan could have been composed of the mill ends your father brought home because the factory couldn't sell them, that your mother gathered to make you a coat she saw Cher wear in an opening number. You could say that she, too, was pushing it, sending a fat kid to kindergarten in a psychedelic duster. Sometimes her immigrant, English-poor insolence was uncomfortable. How she'd yank off a button dangling from a blouse and make you ask the manager for a discount. But what bliss to be ignorant of the ways of the land. To do as you please.

You & Louise Bourgeois's *The Fragile*

"Are they all boobs?" some guy asks at the entrance to the show. Yes, from
the moment you are ten years old and a man remarks, Your garbanzos are
swelling. Or a guy at work asks if your areolas are dark like those of other
Hispanic girls he's known. Or, despite all the contraptions to keep you
from bouncing down the street, you are a crude drawing, ready to topple
with your gazongas into the unfurled tongue dripping with saliva. "Look,
a spider tit!" exclaims another art critic. You want to either strangle him or
whisper firmly, "Kneel before what is holy." And while he is on his knees,
tell him how you come home eager to fold your arms behind your back in
a silent prayer that is the unclasping of the bra. To rub the underwire's
impression and lift the cups into the air like birds. How, braless, you groan
into the safety of your home, *¡Ay, Virgen Santa!* And, wineglass in hand,
meditate on the image of your nipple popping out of your baby's wet lips
as she falls asleep, like a roulette wheel's pointer. How the nightly ritual
erects a feel-good invisible fence that zaps the memory of lip-smack and
heh-heh-heh and ☺. Only then can the gentle lips of your lover kiss each
nipple good night, the cut of his teeth keep them awake.

You & "The Breast"

By now you know the story: an English professor awoke one morning to find himself transformed, like Kafka's Gregor, into something unthinkable, something so unlike who he was. In his case, not a beetle, but a breast. Young, perfectly round, its nipple erect. What if he had become, instead, a breast at ease in middle age, the nipple sure of its opinion but not in constant need to give it? In this room with a turret, where the story was written, you are not turned on but troubled by the memory of your mother in her last years pushed around in a wheelchair, braless. Did it feel like freedom or resignation to no longer have to roust the girls up and about or make them unwilling interlocutors? For the nursing home this was mainly convenience. With so much to do, why harness old women who've wandered off a darkened stage? Your mother, who never answered the door without a girdle, much less a bra. What if the breast had been delicate and shallow, a bead of water trembling on the paddle of a thirsty cactus? Flat as a mesa, scarred like an arroyo? Or why not two breasts, one a full cup larger from having nursed too long in the same position while writing recommendation letters? You lean back and stare at the ceiling above the desk, its concentric circles punctuated in the middle by a round light fixture that teardrops into a nipple, and around the nipple a ragged areola of desiccated wings. One understands when entering a room that others have been there before. But this room is never just itself, it is always a story that hovers over your own. What if the nipple had sprouted a hair and, given the professor's lack of hands, remained forever un-plucked? What if the nipple had been inverted and not, as the story goes, phallic? A breast leaking milk, its infected ducts hard and throbbing under a cabbage leaf? The domed ceiling has two cracks like veins under pale skin. On the roof, where the pointed end of the turret lives, is another breast whose nipple pulls energy from the center of the desk to its weathervane. It's hard to get a signal beneath it; you have to sit on the bed to text a friend whose father died yesterday. "I didn't get a chance to say goodbye," she writes. And, "Fuck capitalism." Framed by the window to the left is a long, thin tree among a thicket. It pushes proudly from its trunk what looks like a breast, because now everything does, but is a scar over a wound called a burl, the result of some type of stress: injury, virus, fungus. Valued for its beauty, this type of scar is often poached, destroying the tree it was trying to protect. A redwood can sprout another redwood from its burl if it thinks it might die. The women in your family, their breasts at any age fall sideward. They never point to future or sky; each, after sex, are waterfalls into canyons.

You & the Raw Bullets

Why the image just now of a bullet entering the mouth? Why call it raw, when it isn't sticky and pink like a turkey meatball, just the usual: gold, and shiny, and cylindrical? What about this bullet is uncooked? Why does it multiply with you in parka or short skirt, swallowing raw bullets as you walk? The images come without assailant, without gun, just the holes the bullets opened, the holes through which they went. Now at the age in which you ride enclosed in glass like the pope or president, you are spitting up the bullets slow-simmered in your own juices. You are shitting them out, feeling them drop in clumps of blood, in the days of bleeding left. But you cannot expel all of them. Some, raw as the day they entered, have expanded their mushroom heads into the flesh, or lodged their hot tips into the taste center of the brain. Will the tongue's first encounter with pomegranate seeds be forever a lost Eden, that fruit of your girlhood, which, also meaning grenade, was perhaps never innocent? Do your own raw bullets come back to you, my friends? Let us legislate the active voice instead. Not, "These bodies have been used as clay pigeons, aluminum cans." But, "Here are the men who pulled the trigger. Look at them."

Industrial Sign Language (You at the Textile Museum)

In the corduroy silence, a woman weaves her hands in the air and laughs. We weren't just operators, she says, but inventors of a secret language the overseers could not read. It was the only way to be heard above din of machine. They thought we were keeping rhythm with warp and weft, that every movement of our wrists kept the thread moving from right to left. But in plain sight, we wove dirty jokes and rumors, recipes for how to have, and not, a baby. What sign didn't she make, in the documentary no visitor watches to the end? What noise could she not overcome, even though overseer is long buried and factory shut down? Did index finger to eye, as the mechanic made his rounds, mean, *Watch out, compañera, that one gets handsy*? Just as on blogs, newspapers, tweets, across entire industries, women are gesturing *ojo ojo ojo*? Did they ever become tired of all the signage? Want to throw up their hands and walk out, let the whole production come to a halt in one tangled mess? For them it probably wasn't an option. Among the weavers, deafness was a chronic condition.

What Good Does It Do You?

No corner more conspicuous than the one children are asked to huddle in for their own protection. It's a drill for when the bad men come looking for them, your daughter explains. Already she's identified who will ruin it for everyone by cracking a joke or crying. And the virtue of compliance: I am very still, Mama, very quiet. Taught at a young age to side with the person who could keep her alive, your mother pressed herself against the fence of the enemy encampment and asked a soldier for bread. She was six, seven? The soldier slipped it through and so she returned every day, and when he'd see her walking down the road, he'd say, "Here comes my girlfriend." Hunger's courting of pity. Pity's dalliance. Maybe there was no fence, no clear division, as so often happens in civil war and in this retelling. Your daughter brings home a book of poems and pictures her class put together. In it there is part heroism, part ache, in rhyme and relations. No fire and ice but lockdown and border agents. Before fighter planes were deployed to eclipse the sun of every child's drawing, your mother as a girl dreamed them dropping bombs on her house. It's not that her mother didn't believe her, it's that the ground was too hard, the basket too heavy, the husband so far away. Your mother never forgot the dream, that once she was an oracle. But what good did it do her when grown-ups went on with business as usual?

At Your Mother's Wake

The funeral director stops you in the hallway by placing his hand deli-cately on your arm. You were headed to the bathroom, to be alone with its enormous vase of fake flowers, to sit on the toilet and not have to dis-cuss body mass index with your uncle. Or listen to your aunt warn you about grave robbers as you kneel in front of your mother's casket: "If you don't take those rings off her hand, they will." Or assure your broth-er's friends you'll try to convince him to become a citizen before the election. Your mother only feet away and those two, canvassing. "It's me, Mike," the funeral director says, "You know, the rockabilly." Gone are his pompadour, his creepers, his bolo tie. He is just a middle-aged guy in a suit, white at the temples. In college he studied political sci-ence and his girlfriend resembled Madonna in her Sean Penn phase. Because you are old friends, he wants you to have—free of charge—the DVD with the montage of your mother's life. Later, as you sit facing the rectangular cutout your mother's coffin will fit into, a brother on each side, you replay the exchange and imagine another life, in which you are married to Mike, the funeral director. And the body lowered into the ground isn't kin but client; this is your professional duty, to stand beside him at every burial. And you have never left New Jersey or put your mother in a nursing home. She lives on the first floor of your two-family house, and on weekends you sit with her on the porch eating her favor-ite pork fried rice and talking about the old neighborhood. "The last time I drove through it looked terrible," you tell her in English, because in this life you can. "La ferretería can't compete with the chain stores on Route 46." She nods and asks, holding up an issue of *People en Español,* "Who's more beautiful, Penelope Cruz or JLo?" Which means, that's not your problem, look how lucky you are to have a hard-working man like Mike, good father to her three perfect grandchildren (two boys, one girl). While keeping the funeral home's books, you write about that life, with insights into the business of death that put you on the map, even though you rarely travel beyond Great Adventure or Seaside Heights. When your mother dies, because even this fantasy cannot escape that fact, getting on the next flight out won't be a problem because you'll be one flight up. Everything will be taken care of, including the best cof-fin at wholesale, and during the wake, you'll escape into Mike's office, its grounding mahogany and calming neutrals, its box of tissues, the kind suffused with soothing drops of aloe vera. And when he finds you there crying, you'll straighten up and say in a still-intact Jersey accent, "Mike, the carpet in here needs a good steaming," and he'll nod and know just what to say, which is nothing.

You Dream of the Closed-Concept Kitchen

At the threshold to sunshine and air, you pull your mother's breath into your lungs and return it to hers. You can't even have your own. This is what it means to be born into the promised land. You must promise to never leave your parents. Remember those commercials for margarine? So modern and so spreadable. So American! Never again would you have to wait for butter to soften, or risk exposing with a dull knife the white underbelly of Wonder Bread's suntan. Once, you opened a window and described a mountain. Leave whenever you want, your mother says. Now eat something.

You in Exile

At twenty-one, you vowed to free the country that was your childhood from tyranny. With sex, dancing, and weed—and an army of conscripted boyfriends—the campaign appeared to be working. Phase One: Destroy its radio towers and presses. Two: Drive its regime to the coast and into the sea. But when your father, then your mother, died, you imposed sanctions on your own grief and resumed your steady gait to work. Because who is ever really punished by a republic of troubled ghosts? Your daughter who refuses to turn off the TV and brush her hair? News from the regime intercepts the signal of the present until it becomes the present. In this pandemic, some exes haven't seen their own parents in so long, or they talk to them through nursing home windows. And you? Your arms have become heavy, your hands. The weight of something unnameable pulling you down. You've stopped dyeing your hair and feeling alive in teen clothes. When will it happen, and to whom and where? You cannot straighten your neck. You miss your father's hands, how he'd rub saliva into it when you'd wake up with a crick. The old remedies die with each human trial. Phase Three. You want to throw things away, who could wear them? In the deepest ocean, delicate slip embroidered with possessive. A future like ash that floats up and away.

Emailing Your Exes

Hi, how are you doing? Sorry to be the cliché in your morning. I hope your face mask is working against big droplets. Do you love the world you are caught in? The wife in finance, the lack of artistic outlet? Still, it's better than living off your talent. Are you still self-conscious about your nose? I've finally lost my derided accent. I said pants, while you said trousers. Remember how you disliked tongue kissers on the subway, their vulgate upsetting your crossword? How you wanted to edify the underclass in the proper hanging of picture frames? God bless you for looking past my museum-shop replicas. You were loved for your introductions, how you murmured *déclassé* into my ear and bound my wrists with a necktie you said was vintage. My skin couldn't tell if it was satin or silk. You said it was an innate skill, but now I know at the summit of my career. Are you dying without me? Did you burn the Polaroids? Remember the time I strapped your painting to the roof of my car and it flew off and down the Henry Hudson? How I risked my life to pick up the pieces, how it could have been a performance? The masses would be grateful for your lessons if they could stay home and read, but they are delivering sushi on wobbly bikes and ringing up kombucha behind plastic shields. The memory of us, in which I sort of hate you, keeps me from despairing at the present losses. This is what resentment, what desire, is good for. You are out there somewhere and I'll never send this. When I yelled *drop dead,* when I wanted to kill you for what you did or said, I was more alive than ever and wanted to feel the big impossible heartache of the one great love promised in the earliest propaganda. But now that death is not a code-switch but our only register, I come to you, my old flame, as if this email were a vaccine against the sadness that mutates, the curve that never flattens.

This Little Catalog You've Been Assembling

Below the headline, "It's 115 Degrees. Is it Death Valley? No, France, and It's Just the Start," a half-page photograph of sunbathers at the Trocadéro Gardens. In it, a young woman in a bikini texts while talking to a friend, both sitting on a small hill with other twentysomethings, the Eiffel Tower at their feet. A red plastic cup rolls down the path, and in the distance, a middle-aged man in a rumpled suit jacket enters from a more temperate past. Contemplating this Impressionist scene, all you can think is, "I'll never wear a two-piece again." It is the article that rouses the requisite dread: chicken manure spontaneously ignites on a farm in Spain and sparks a wildfire! Were there no photos for the jump page besides a hot guy in Pamplona carrying a fan? The plan this morning was to write about the stranger who tried to kiss you the second the elevator doors met, but aren't there bigger fish to lose to extinction, too many languages? Perhaps this little catalog you've been assembling isn't all that urgent when in a heatwave the autobahn can buckle and send your Volkswagen surfing. When there are things more traumatizing than some guy calling out across a subway platform, "Look at that fat pussy!" You want to shout back, years later: GREENLAND AND ALASKA ARE MELTING! Once, in an elevator, a man confided that standing idle with others in that space made him anxious. "Should I whip out a deck of cards," he asked, "and propose a game?" Whatever you've been dealt, stranger, this elevator and everyone in it are going straight down.

Screw You, ICE

In the name you hear a lathe on which a story is carved and shaped and smoothed. Tornillo, from the Latin tornus, to turn. A thing that can be loosened or tightened, that lets reading glasses be folded and put in a pocket. Or in its more rudimentary form made a simple job of extracting oil from an olive, and during the Spanish Inquisition, confession from a thumb. "Mientras más hilos hay en un tornillo, mayor sirve su propósito." But the town of Tornillo was likely named for the spiral-shaped mesquite pods that grow there and can be boiled into a syrup. How many remember the name now that the detention center is closed, out of the papers? Because elsewhere in this country the children are still afraid. They hang from bunk beds multicolored threads saved from the obligatory craft. A fringe to diffuse harsh light, to conjure a mother's face, moments before she is pulled away. In encampments on the other side of the border, where they wait for months, refused entry, more children huddle around a kind volunteer who has brought a math sheet to teach them subtraction. Add to the count the children missing. The problem is a history you turn and turn as if a chunk of metal in a lathe. What you get for the effort is a screw you place on the table to contemplate. In every groove, progress is implied. The piles of filings easily swept away would tell otherwise.

R U ok?! (8/3/2019)

Checking in. Let me know you're not anywhere near Cielo Vista Mall, please. Active shooter in the area. Just heard about the shooting in El Paso. You guys all ok? I just read there was a shooting in an El Paso mall. Assuming you're all fine, but just checking. Si usted y su familia están en El Paso, espero que estén a salvo. Safe and sound? r u guys ok?! You guys ok? Thinking of you, and El Paso, and our American addiction to gun violence. ¿Cómo están? Qué tragedia horrible. Les mando muchos besos. Querida, are you all ok? Sending ♡ and cariño. Just reading about El Paso. Sending all my 💕. Colleagues, I hope you and yours are all safe ♡. Just want to tell everyone I know that I love them. Xxoo I hope you and your family are safe. My dear, I'm sorry to text you to ask if you are all safe and sound but I love you and I must. This is horrific. Please tell me you were nowhere near a Walmart today ⚖. Hey fam, thinking of you. 💔 for El Chuco. Are you ok? How are you doing, hermana. I miss you. Terribly upsetting situation in El Paso. My heart goes out to you all. ¿Cómo están ustedes? ¿Estás bien y tú familia y conocidos? 🏥 muy doloroso. No paro de llorar.

You Choose the World: A Poetics

Called inside by the consonance of the familiar, you down the irremediable loneliness of something long gone, its bootleg liquor. What if instead you remained in the mosquito lushness of the present, letting your arms and legs feel the itch spread toward the world's edges? What if your discomfort became one with the world's, the itchiness unable to resolve either/or? Your daughter says, "I'm itching it," as if the itch were self-imposed. And it is. Who else to blame? You cannot love the world enough, so take a deep breath, exhale the frightened girl no one knows exists. And at the sound of your father returning from work, his black hair undulating beneath your eyelids, suck her back in. Feel now buoyant, now desperate. Push your body to the surface, cough into the room. In the unsettled dust of another windstorm, be of service to the child who arrives alone. To the man who carries court papers through the airport in a Ziploc bag. The woman who nurses her newborn in a cage, unable to lie down. Let the itch release and multiply, love the world. Be for it. Kill Mother and Father's scene, raise the scrim, thin as breath. Will it be unbearable? To know you are not alone but with the world, that not everything broken can be repaired? Your body will always be placed at a long glass table, asked to choose between opposing forces: at one end a refugee pulled from a boat by one arm, at the other, the origin story you tell yourself, safe and far from harm. Dwell in the negotiations. Now that you are an orphan, family is of your choosing. As always, it will be imperfect.

You are the you of this poem, mon amour.

—DAVID SHAPIRO

Acknowledgments

A big, whopping GRACIAS to the following editors and journals for publishing earlier versions of these poems:

The Adroit Journal (Peter LaBerge): Would You?

American Poetry Review (Elizabeth Scanlon): You, Escape Artist; Your Mother's Advice; You, Glistening in the Meadow; You in Palazzo Pants; You & "The Breast"

Aster(ix) (Angie Cruz): You & the Pendulum; You to the Future; Your Daughter Refashions the Flag into a Crop Top

The Best American Poetry 2019 (Major Jackson): You & the Raw Bullets

Chicago Review: (Hannah Brooks-Motl): You in Cutoffs; You, a Hand, Another; You, the Bourgeoisie; You & the Banker

The Georgia Review (Soham Patel): R U ok?! (8/3/2019); Industrial Sign Language (You at the Textile Museum); You & Louise Bourgeois's *The Fragile*; You Were an Asshole

Harper's Magazine (Ben Lerner): How It Started, How It's Going

The Literary Review (Michael Morse): You & the Donkey Cart; What Good Does It Do You?; You Lie; You, Amateur Interpreter

Poem-a-Day (Dawn Lundy Martin & Monica Youn): You & the Raw Bullets; You Rode a Loop

The Texas Review (Ginger Ko): You, the Body & the Book; You, Supplicant; What Does Your Daughter Wish For?; What Did You Dream?; What You Knew About Virginity

To those who helped *YOU* along: Sylvia Aguilar, Andrea Blancas Beltrán, Susan Briante, Andrea Cote Botero, Angie Cruz, Annie Ernaux, Suzi García, Carmen Giménez, Richard Greenfield, Anna Maria Hong, Katie Peterson, Elizabeth Powell, Kristin Prevallet, Elizabeth Spackman, and Roberto Tejada.

To Coffee House Press and Erika Stevens.

To my colleagues and friends in El Paso who do the miraculous thing of writing while also meeting the exigencies of academia.

To Bill Clark at Literarity for hand-selling my books to unsuspecting customers. Hurray for independent booksellers.

To Yaddo for giving me a respite from grocery shopping, which I'm very bad at, and allowing *YOU* to take shape.

To my mother and father, who live on in these poems. And to my brothers, Carlos and José.

To Jeff & Raquel, for reminding me daily that poetry is who I am. You make this life possible.

And to the writers and artists whose work, cited below, enriches this book:

Eleanor Antin, interview in *Originals: American Women Artists* by Eleanor Munro (New York: Da Capo Press, 2000)

Ingeborg Bachmann's "[How Much Longer? Not Much Longer]," translated by Peter Filkins, in *Darkness Spoken: The Collected Poems* (Brookline, MA: Zephyr Press, 2006)

Louise Bourgeois, no. 8 of 9 in the series *What Is the Shape of This Problem?* (New York: Galerie Lelong, 1999)

Sor Juana Inés de la Cruz's "Hombres necios que acusáis"

Cathleen Medwick's *Teresa of Avila: The Progress of a Soul* (New York: Knopf, 1999)

Yoko Ono's "Cut Piece" performance, as filmed by Albert and David Maysles on March 21, 1965, at Carnegie Recital Hall, New York

Mary Ruefle's "Pause," from *My Private Property* (Seattle & New York: Wave Books, 2016)

David Shapiro's "You Are the You," from *After a Lost Original* (Woodstock, NY: The Overlook Press, 1994)

Sara Uribe's "Poema en que la enunciante se rehúsa a continuar siendo una ama de casa triste, una oficinista poco comprometida, una autómata de la ubicuidad doméstica, una reinita cualquiera," from her book *Un montón de escritura para nada* (Mexico City: Dharma Books, 2019)

Cecilia Vicuña's painting *Amaranta* (oil on canvas, 1972–2021)

William Carlos Williams's *Paterson* (New York: New Directions, 1963)

Ludwig Wittgenstein's *Philosophical Investigations,* fourth ed., translated by G. E. M. Anscombe, P. M. S. Hacker, and Joachim Schulte (West Sussex, UK: Wiley-Blackwell, 2009)

A Note

The poem "R U ok?! (9/3/2019)" is a found poem of collective worry and fear, collaged from some of the texts I received from friends and family as news began to emerge of an active shooter in El Paso. It is in memory of the twenty-three mothers, fathers, daughters, sons, brothers, sisters, husbands, wives, partners, nieces, nephews, grandchildren, aunts, uncles, cousins, and friends who were murdered by a white supremacist at a Walmart in El Paso. It is also for their loved ones, who would never receive a response telling them everything was okay.

Coffee House Press began as a small letterpress operation in 1972 and has grown into an internationally renowned nonprofit publisher of literary fiction, essay, poetry, and other work that doesn't fit neatly into genre categories.

Coffee House is both a publisher and an arts organization. Through our *Books in Action* program and publications, we've become interdisciplinary collaborators and incubators for new work and audience experiences. Our vision for the future is one where a publisher is a catalyst and connector.

LITERATURE
is not the same thing as
PUBLISHING

Funder Acknowledgments

Coffee House Press is an internationally renowned independent book publisher and arts nonprofit based in Minneapolis, MN; through its literary publications and *Books in Action* program, Coffee House acts as a catalyst and connector—between authors and readers, ideas and resources, creativity and community, inspiration and action.

Coffee House Press books are made possible through the generous support of grants and donations from corporations, state and federal grant programs, family foundations, and the many individuals who believe in the transformational power of literature. This activity is made possible by the voters of Minnesota through a Minnesota State Arts Board Operating Support grant, thanks to the legislative appropriation from the Arts and Cultural Heritage Fund. Coffee House also receives major operating support from the Amazon Literary Partnership, Jerome Foundation, Literary Arts Emergency Fund, McKnight Foundation, and the National Endowment for the Arts (NEA). To find out more about how NEA grants impact individuals and communities, visit www.arts.gov.

Coffee House Press receives additional support from Bookmobile; the Buckley Charitable Fund; Dorsey & Whitney LLP; the Gaea Foundation; the Schwab Charitable Fund; and the U.S. Bank Foundation.

The Publisher's Circle of Coffee House Press

Publisher's Circle members make significant contributions to Coffee House Press's annual giving campaign. Understanding that a strong financial base is necessary for the press to meet the challenges and opportunities that arise each year, this group plays a crucial part in the success of Coffee House's mission.

Recent Publisher's Circle members include many anonymous donors, Kathy Arnold, Patricia A. Beithon, Andrew Brantingham & Rita Farmer, Kelli & Dave Cloutier, Theodore Cornwell, Mary Ebert & Paul Stembler, Kamilah Foreman, Eva Galiber, Jocelyn Hale & Glenn Miller Charitable Fund of the Minneapolis Foundation, Roger Hale & Nor Hall, William Hardacker, Randy Hartten & Ron Lotz, Carl & Heidi Horsch, Amy L. Hubbard & Geoffrey J. Kehoe Fund of the St. Paul & Minnesota Foundation, Kenneth & Susan Kahn, the Kenneth Koch Literary Estate, Cinda Kornblum, the Lenfestey Family Foundation, Sarah Lutman & Rob Rudolph, Carol & Aaron Mack, Gillian McCain, Mary & Malcolm McDermid, Daniel N. Smith III & Maureen Millea Smith, Vance Opperman, Mr. Pancks' Fund in memory of Graham Kimpton, Alan Polsky, Robin Preble, Steve Smith, Paul Thissen, Grant Wood, and Margaret Wurtele.

For more information about the Publisher's Circle and other ways to support Coffee House Press books, authors, and activities, please visit www.coffeehousepress.org/pages/donate or contact us at info@coffeehousepress.org.

Rosa Alcalá has published three previous books of poetry, most recently *MyOTHER TONGUE*. She has been awarded fellowships and grants from the Foundation for Contemporary Arts, Harvard's Woodberry Poetry Room, Yaddo, MacDowell, Fundación Valparaíso, and the National Endowment for the Arts. Her translation and editorial work include *New & Selected Poems of Cecilia Vicuña* and *Spit Temple: The Selected Performances of Cecilia Vicuña,* runner-up for the 2013 PEN Translation Award. She is the De Wetter Endowed Chair in Poetry at the University of Texas at El Paso's Department of Creative Writing and Bilingual MFA Program.

YOU was designed by Bookmobile Design & Digital Publisher Services. Text is set in Minion Pro.